SOLO Wildlife

Polar Bear

Written and illustrated
by David Kennett

SOLOS

For Yoshie with love and appreciation

First published in Australia by Omnibus Books 2000
This edition published in the UK under licence from
Omnibus Books by
Southwood Books Limited, 2001.

Text and illustrations copyright © David Kennett 2000
Cover design by Lyn Mitchell
Typeset by Clinton Ellicott, Adelaide
Printed in Singapore

ISBN 1 903207 33 9

The polar bear

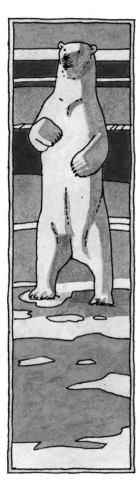

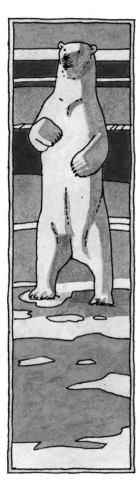 is a warm-blooded animal

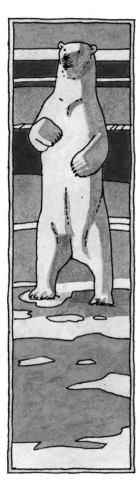 is one of the most dangerous bears on earth

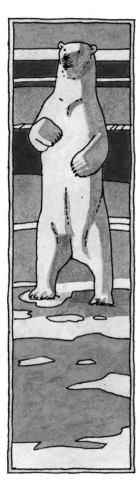 can be as heavy as a small car

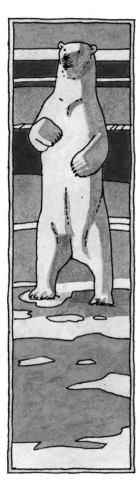 has been a protected animal since 1973

 can be hunted only by people of the Arctic using traditional weapons.

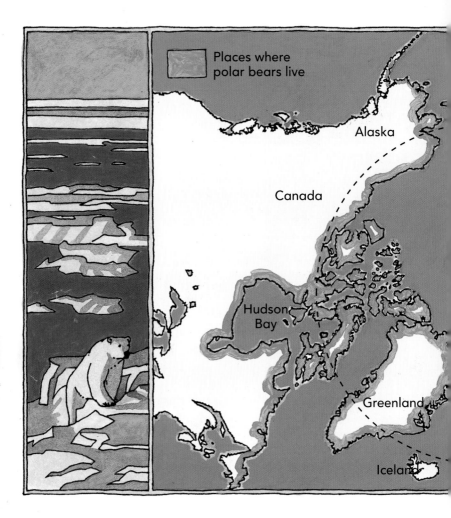

Places where
polar bears live

Alaska

Canada

Hudson
Bay

Greenland

Iceland

At the very north of the world, around
the North Pole, is a place of ice and
frozen seas called the Arctic Circle. In
winter, the Arctic is dark.

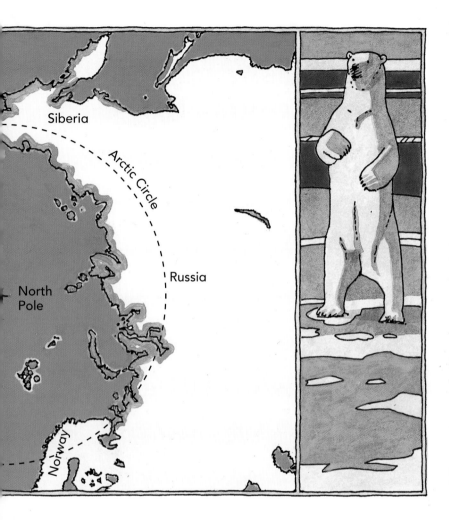

Wind howls across the snow and everything freezes. Humans find it hard to live in such a cold place, but polar bears live there easily.

A polar bear is one of the biggest bears in the world. It is also one of the biggest meat-eating land animals.

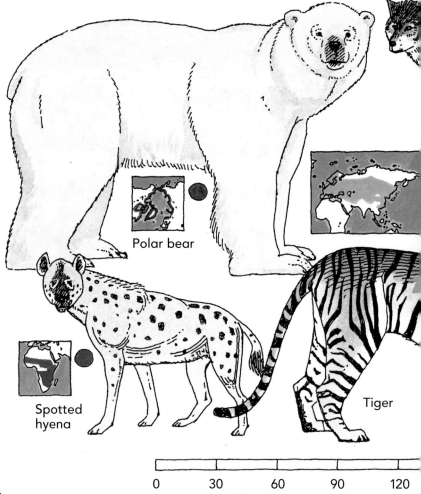

Polar bear

Spotted hyena

Tiger

0   30   60   90   120

These animals eat the flesh of other animals. They are called carnivores. The maps show where each animal lives.

Wolf

Lion

Badger

River otter

A male polar bear is bigger and
heavier than a female polar bear.

This male measures 2.6 metres from its tail to its nose and 1.2 metres from the top of its shoulder to the ground.

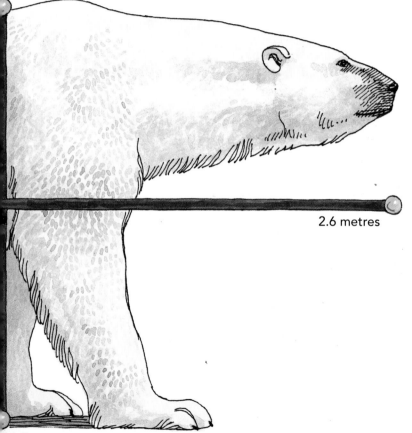

2.6 metres

1.2 metres

A house cat weighs about three and a half kilograms. You would need about 129 and a half cats to make up the weight of this male polar bear.
It weighs 453 kilograms.

A big male can weigh as much as 680 kilograms.

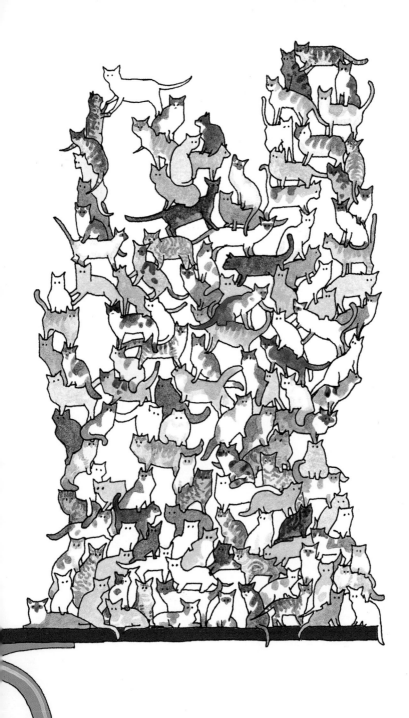

When an adult male polar bear stands on his hind legs, his head can be three metres above the ground.

3 metres

No one knows how long polar bears
live in the wild, but in a zoo they have
been known to live for as long as
40 years.

Many other meat-eating animals such as wolves and tigers will fight one another over territories. Polar bears do not fight over territories. They wander over a large area.

14

In winter, an Arctic fox will choose a bear to follow, so that it can live on the food the bear leaves behind.
It will fight other foxes that try to 'adopt' his bear. A fox will defend his bear as if it was his territory.

In winter, polar bears spend much of their time on pack ice. This is a layer of very thick ice that covers the sea. The area of pack ice is much larger in winter than it is in summer.

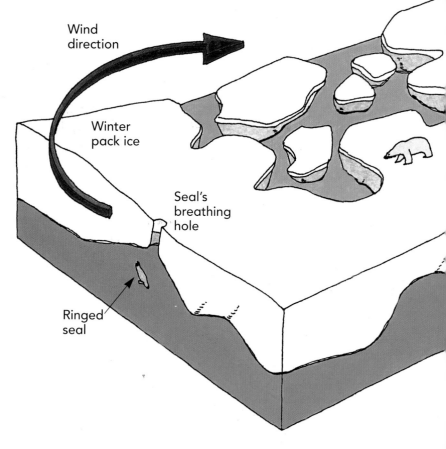

Wind direction

Winter pack ice

Seal's breathing hole

Ringed seal

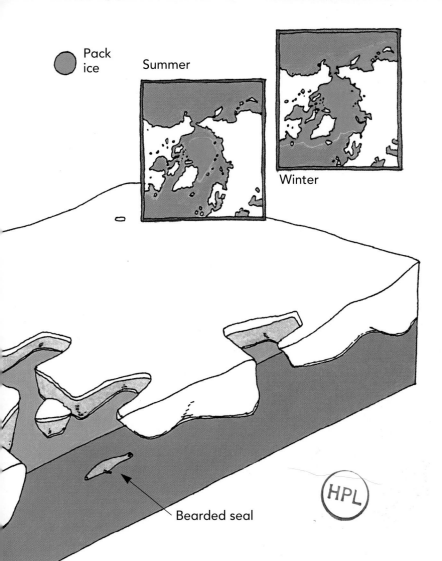

Pack ice

Summer

Winter

Bearded seal

HPL

The wind in the Arctic keeps the pack ice moving. If a polar bear wants to stay in one place, then it must keep moving.

Polar bears will eat anything they can catch. They eat small land mammals like lemmings. They even eat stranded whales. Their main food is seals.

Hooded seal

Bearded seal

Ringed seals are the polar bear's main prey, but they also kill and eat hooded, bearded, and banded seals. The maps show where these seals live.

Banded seal

Ringed seal

A polar bear can smell a ringed seal pup in its birth den under the snow. At birth, a ringed seal pup weighs about 5 kilograms.

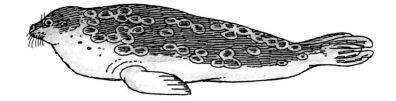

A big, hungry polar bear will eat up to 68 kilograms of food at one meal.

This is as much as the weight of one adult ringed seal, or 13 and three-fifths seal pups.

Polar bears hunt seals by waiting
quietly by a seal's breathing hole.
When the seal comes up for air, the
bear catches it and pulls it up on to
the ice.

When there are many seals, a polar
bear will catch one every four or
five days.

A polar bear once ate 1000 eider duck eggs in one meal. An eider duck egg is twice as big as a hen's egg.

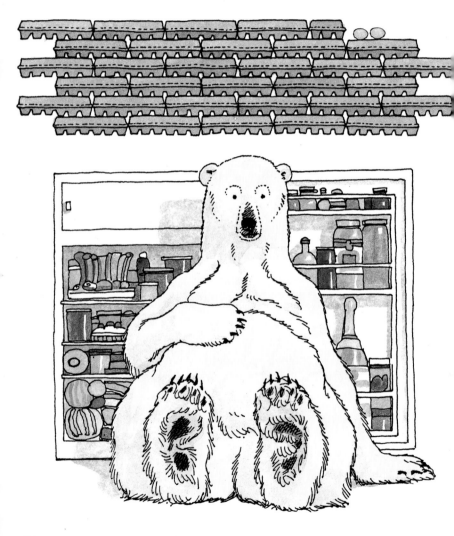

If you invited that polar bear to breakfast, you would have to feed it 2000 hen eggs, which is nearly 167 cartons of eggs!

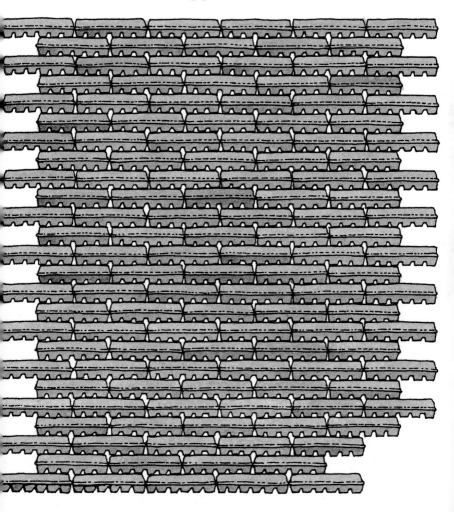

A polar bear's foot can be
30 centimetres wide. The body length
of a house cat is 50 centimetres.
Three-fifths of this cat would be in
shadow if they ever met.

Because they are so wide, the polar bear's feet help spread its weight. This makes walking on snow and ice easier.

Humans use snowshoes to help spread their weight when they are walking on snow.

A polar bear has very thick hair around its footpads. This helps its feet grip well in the ice and snow.

To stalk its prey the polar bear needs to walk very quietly. Hairy feet soften the sound of its footsteps.

A polar bear has black skin. Black absorbs heat, and helps the bear stay warm. Underneath its skin is a layer of fat up to 10 centimetres thick.

Fur

Skin

Fat

Fat protects the polar bear from the
cold and helps it to float when it is
swimming. When food is scarce, the
bear can survive on this fat.

Polar bears are very good swimmers. They use their broad front paws in a dog paddle. These animals can swim without stopping for 160 kilometres.

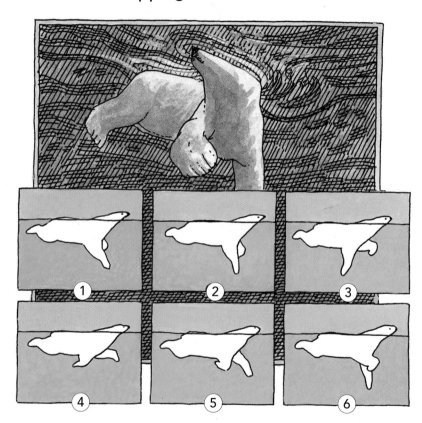

The toes on the polar bear's front paws are webbed. This helps it to swim.

Polar bears also swim well underwater. They can stay underwater for two minutes before coming up for air.

On land, a polar bear will sometimes hunt and kill a young walrus.

When they are both in the water, an adult walrus can kill a polar bear by stabbing it with its tusks.

Winter and summer are much longer at the North and South Pole than they are in other places on earth.

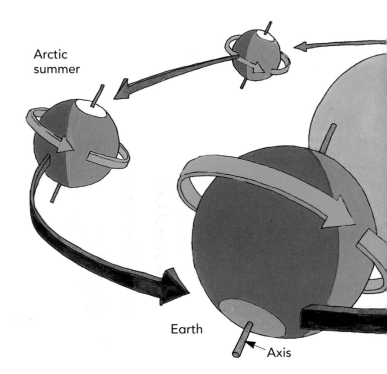

Arctic summer

Earth

Axis

The earth spins on its axis. This is an imaginary pole going through the earth. The axis is always tilted.

The earth takes 24 hours to spin round once on its axis. It takes one year for the earth to travel all the way round the sun.

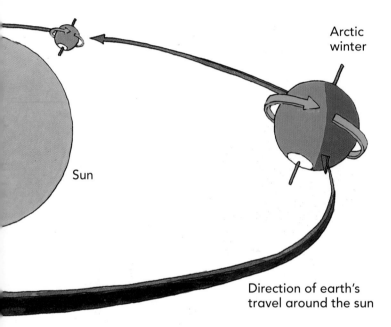

Arctic winter

Sun

Direction of earth's travel around the sun

For half of the year the Arctic is tilted away from the sun. This is the Arctic winter. For the other half of the year the Arctic is tilted towards the sun. This is the Arctic summer.

In summer, the pack ice melts in some parts of the Arctic, and polar bears must live closer to the land.

Away from the ice, they cannot catch seals, and they may not be fast enough to catch other prey.

For many animals, there is plenty of food to eat in summer, but for polar bears it is hard. They can survive on stored body fat, but they often lose weight.

A female polar bear does not breed until she is four or five years old. Then she can have cubs every two years.

When females are busy with their cubs, they will not mate.

Male polar bears will fight each other for a female.

When the male polar bear has won his female he stays with her for about one week and they mate often.

As soon as the female bear becomes pregnant, she chases the male bear away. The female raises her cubs alone.

In autumn, the pregnant female polar bear digs a den deep in the snow on a hillside. Polar bear cubs are born in winter inside this den.

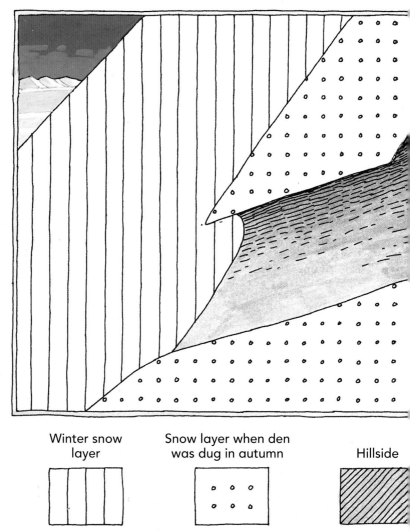

Winter snow layer

Snow layer when den was dug in autumn

Hillside

Winter snow covers the entrance to the den. The temperature outside drops well below freezing, but the mother and her cubs stay warm inside.

Polar bear cubs are very small when
they are born. They are about the size
of a rat, and weigh about 680 grams.
They could not survive alone.

The mother bear does not eat or drink in the den. She does not urinate or make droppings. Her stored body fat provides milk for the cubs.

Polar bear mothers keep the den clean by covering the cubs' urine and droppings with a fresh layer of snow scraped from the top and sides of the den.

The female polar bear can be inside the den for as long as seven months. Her heartbeat slows right down. This means she uses less energy and can survive on her stored body fat.

When the mother finally leaves the den with her cubs, she has lost most of her body weight. She has eaten nothing for many months.

Cubs usually stay with their mothers for two years. She teaches them to hunt for their food.

It may be that the Inuit people learned many things from studying polar bears. Their igloos are warm inside, just like a polar bear's nursing den.

The Inuit hunted seals by waiting
quietly by the seal's breathing hole,
just as a polar bear does.

In the past, most people would never have seen a polar bear. They were so rare that kings were sometimes given them as special gifts.

Hunters trapped polar bears and took them far away from their homes in the Arctic.

King Ptolemy of Egypt had a polar
bear that once walked through the
streets at the front of a great parade.

More than 1000 years ago, two polar bears were given to the emperor of Japan.

The polar bear belonging to the sultan El Kamil of Damascus was taken every morning to hunt fish in the river.

When white people first came to the
Arctic, it seemed that there was no
limit to the wildlife there. It did not
take long for hunters to drive many
animals close to extinction.

Now hunting is controlled by law. Polar bears are no longer threatened with extinction. Many tourists travel to the Arctic just to look at these wonderful animals.

Glossary

adopt • choose or make your own.

carnivore • an animal that eats meat as its main food.

extinct • (of an animal) an animal that has died out.

hind legs • back legs.

igloo • a house made with blocks of ice.

mammal • animal whose young is fed on milk from the mother's body.

pack ice • a thick layer of frozen water that covers the sea at the North and the South Pole.

predator • animal that hunts and kills other animals for its food.

prey • an animal that is hunted and killed by another animal.

protected animal • an animal that people are not allowed to hunt or kill.

stranded (whale) • a whale that has come too close to land and cannot swim back to deeper water.

territory • the area of land that an animal hunts in and defends against other animals.

traditional • something from the past that belongs to a group of people.

urinate • make urine.

warm-blooded animal • an animal whose blood temperature stays at between 36 and 44 degrees Celsius in cold or hot weather. Humans keep their temperature at this level in winter by wearing warm clothes.

weapon • a tool for fighting or killing.

🐻 Index